Verse Mapping

BIBLE STUDY Journal

Deepen Your Bible Reading and Unpack the Meaning of Scripture

KRISTY CAMBRON

THOMAS NELSON
Since 1798

Verse Mapping Bible Study Journal

© 2020 by Kristy Cambron

Published in Nashville, Tennessee, by Thomas Nelson. Thomas Nelson is a registered trademark of HarperCollins Christian Publishing, Inc.

Published in association with Books & Such Literary Management, 52 Mission Circle, Suite 122, PMB 170, Santa Rosa, California 95409-5370, www.booksandsuch.com.

All Scripture quotations, unless otherwise indicated, are taken from The Holy Bible, New International Version®, NIV®. Copyright © 1973, 1978, 1984, 2011 by Biblica, Inc.™ Used by permission. All rights reserved worldwide.

Scripture quotations marked NKJV are taken from the New King James Version®. © 1982 by Thomas Nelson. Used by permission. All rights reserved.

Study Support Examples sections are excerpted from *NIV Biblical Theology Study Bible*. Copyright © 2015, 2018. Published by Zondervan, Grand Rapids, Michigan.

Photo on page 107 © Shutterstock.

ISBN 978-0-310-12401-6

Second Printing March 2021 / Printed in China

Contents

verse mapping 101 GUIDE

Steps to Study the Bible
Like Never Before

WHY VERSE MAPPING?

Let's be honest—does anyone else have difficulty understanding Scripture? *(Waving hand over here . . .)*

Do you want to do more than just read—you actually want to research and apply what's in the Bible to your life today? *(Me too! Waving again.)*

Are you looking for a fellowship community where you can read, learn, explore, and map the Word of God together? *(Still here!)*

If this is you too, and you love unpacking the context of the Scriptures you're reading, but you want to do it in a super-simple way—looking at the Hebrew/Greek translations, finding connections in the Word, and learning as much as you can from your time with the Holy Spirit—then get ready. . . . You've just joined the community study that will inspire, encourage, and unlock your understanding of the Word of God!

WHAT IS VERSE MAPPING?

Verse mapping isn't new. It's been a topic of conversation for years. You'll find endless examples with a simple online search. And you guessed it—Bible journaling images and methods are popping up all over social media. But what is verse mapping? Who's doing it? And can it really help you understand the Word more clearly?

First things first . . .

definition: *Verse mapping is a method of studying the historical context, transliteration, translation, connotation, and theological framework of a verse (or section of verses) in the Bible.*

Plain and simple? Verse mapping is getting real about studying the Bible. All of it. It's not just reading. It's researching everything you can in a verse to learn more about who God is and how He wants to speak to you through His Word. In short? It's serious study.

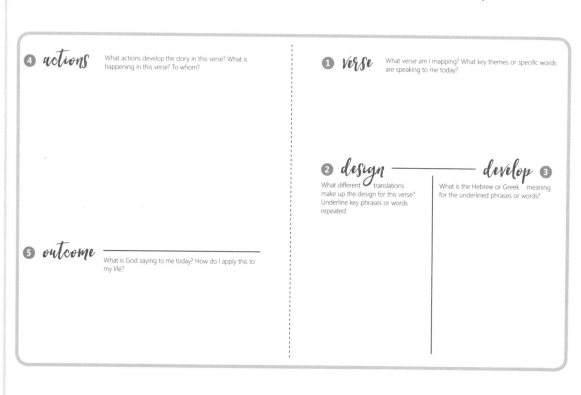

4 actions
What actions develop the story in this verse? What is happening in this verse? To whom?

1 verse
What verse am I mapping? What key themes or specific words are speaking to me today?

2 design
What different translations make up the design for this verse? Underline key phrases or words repeated.

develop 3
What is the Hebrew or Greek meaning for the underlined phrases or words?

5 outcome
What is God saying to me today? How do I apply this to my life?

HOW-TO FOR BEGINNERS

What qualifies me to do this kind of study?

If you're not a seminary-trained theologian by education, don't worry—verse mapping is for anyone with a heart to know the Word of God more.

What matters is not how much knowledge you have before you begin, but where the experience takes you. Verse mapping will inspire you to dig into the Word of God in individual study and in a group setting like never before. The Holy Spirit is your teacher and companion in this study; it's not the *what* you bring to the table that qualifies you—it's *Who*. And He's going to make sure you learn no matter where you begin.

What are the rules?

- **Rule #1:** If you can't back up your conclusions or thoughts with Scripture, then you can't write it down. Everything is fair game in studying *as long as God said it first*. (In other words, don't make anything up and don't assume you know what something means— back it up with Scripture or go back and find the *real* answer.)

- **Rule #2:** Make it personal. This is your journal and your study time with God. More than anything, let God meet you in this unique and intimate space and speak to you.

- **Rule #3:** Keep to your preferences for verse mapping—if you like to highlight . . . if you like to use a specific marker/pen color . . . or if you like to circle or underline key words and phrases. Do what feels intuitive for you.

There's no structurally right or wrong way to verse map. This particular study is structured working from right to left (a documentation page on the right, notes page on the left), and top to bottom. Once you've gathered the tools and mastered the confidence to apply what you've learned, it's up to you how your journal will look. Focus on the process and the way of this study method. Learn how to read and ask at the same time, and then go find the answers.

GATHERING AND GETTING STARTED

This section is quick. It's all about gathering a handful of tools and readying your heart for Him.

What you will need

Whether you're at a desk in your home office, at the local coffee shop, or on the go, verse mapping is a study method that will move with you. In fact, you probably already carry everything you need just about anywhere you go:

- **Journal:** Verse Mapping study guide with blank maps, or a notebook with blank pages.

- **Markers/pens:** Specific colors of markers or pens aren't required. This is personal.

- **Bible:** Or a Bible app on a smart device (to look up various translations).

- **Concordance:** Select a concordance with Hebrew/Greek dictionaries. I recommend *The NIV Exhaustive Bible Concordance, Third Edition* from Zondervan, but you can also find the information online. If you don't have one—or if you're not able to carry one with you— you can also find this information on your smart device.

- **Time (varies):** While it's a requirement, the time you block on your calendar is *up to you.* Study time is on the honor system between you and God. If you have five minutes today and an hour tomorrow, dedicate what time you can, when you can. It's all about communion with Him.

Study Prompt:

Time is a big factor. You may have others who depend on you either inside your home, outside it, or both—and that can cut into the time you're able to study. If finding study *time* is a struggle that becomes a burden, then add that into the next step and pray about it. Eventually, you won't have to carve out time in the Word; it will be what your heart craves first, and most. The time to study will follow the passion to learn.

Prayer

This is a Holy Spirit-led study. So pray. Talk to Him. Ask Him to reveal more of who He is through your verse mapping journey.

The Holy Spirit must be the active guide in any time of study. Do whatever works to invite Him into your study space (listen to worship music, close the door, turn off all sound). Pray before every single time you open your Bible and intentionally seek deeper and clearer understanding of what you will read.

MAPPING 101

A comprehensive guide to change-your-life study time with God.

The process is simple. Each of the following words corresponds to a section on your verse map. Here's what you do (after you pray!):

- **Verse:** Select and write your verse(s) to map. Include the translation.

- **Design:** Write your verse(s) in two to four different translations. Identify key words or phrases that stand out among the varying translations.

- **Develop:** Look up key words or phrases in Hebrew/Greek. Write down definitions, synonyms, and root words. Discover any underlying meaning(s) in verse(s) and note it. (See the Reference and Resource Guide at the back of this study guide if you need help with where to look words up.)

- **Actions:** Research and document the people, places, and the context referenced. Ask: Who? What? Where? When? Why? How? Note connections to other concepts in Scripture you are familiar with and/or find in your research.

- **Outcome:** Write a one- to two-sentence summary of what you've learned. Anchor the verse you mapped to your life. This is the treasured truth the map brought you to.

That's it—five simple steps to change-your-life study time with God! All set? Let's map.

THE MAP

4 *actions* What actions develop the story in this verse? What is happening in this verse? To whom?

1 *verse* What verse am I mapping? What key themes or specific words are speaking to me today?

> WRITE YOUR VERSE(S) –
>
> *WHAT IS THE HOLY SPIRIT TEACHING ME?*

2 *design* What different translations make up the design for this verse? Underline key phrases or words repeated.

develop **3** What is the Hebrew or Greek meaning for the underlined phrases or words?

5 *outcome* What is God saying to me today? How do I apply this to my life?

---

1 *verse*

Select your verse(s)

Everything in your map will hinge on what verse(s) you select. Whether you're reading through an entire book of the Bible or moving around through a verse(s) of a specific theme, this is where you choose what your path will be for your study time. A few questions to ask yourself as you read:

- *What grabs me when I read it?*

- *What themes do I see?*

- *What question(s) do I have about what I just read?*

Write your verse(s)

If something stands out, then you can be sure that's your verse(s) for the day. Select it and write it down.

This study is formatted for use with the New International Version of the Bible. However, you can choose which translation(s) you prefer most. Once you've selected the verse(s) you'll map, write it in your preferred translation. (Remember, you'll document it in at least two to four other translations next.)

Study Prompt:

What verse are you mapping? What key themes or specific words are speaking to you today?

- *What's on your heart today?* If you're facing a difficult circumstance, or find yourself in an unexpected path in your own story with God, select a verse(s) that speaks to the theme of your heart for today.

- *What's that word?* If you're reading Scripture and something jumps off the page—a word you don't recognize, a city you've never heard of, or a phrase you don't quite understand—this is a good indication it might be your verse(s) to map for the day.

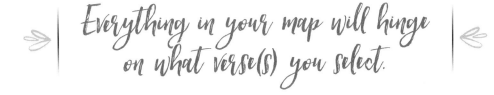

Everything in your map will hinge on what verse(s) you select.

Study Prompt:

What gets lost in translation? How do the different translations present the same ideas or biblical principles?

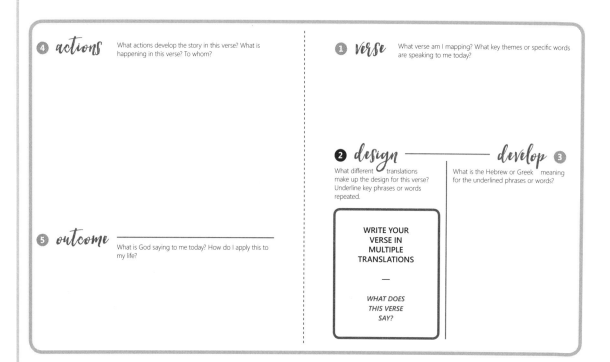

4 actions — What actions develop the story in this verse? What is happening in this verse? To whom?

1 verse — What verse am I mapping? What key themes or specific words are speaking to me today?

2 design — **develop 3**

What different translations make up the design for this verse? Underline key phrases or words repeated.

What is the Hebrew or Greek meaning for the underlined phrases or words?

WRITE YOUR VERSE IN MULTIPLE TRANSLATIONS

—

WHAT DOES THIS VERSE SAY?

5 outcome — What is God saying to me today? How do I apply this to my life?

2 design

The *design* identifies what the verse is calling attention to by comparing translations. The *design* calls out similar word choice, repetition of words, phrases, and/or aspects of grammar common across multiple translations. It brings to light what the verse is saying that cannot be lost to translation, and what may stand out as translation specific. Anything here could trigger a question or path for further investigation.

Write your verse(s)—or selected phrase(s)—in two to four additional translations. Underline, circle, or highlight key phrases or words that may be repeated across multiple translations.

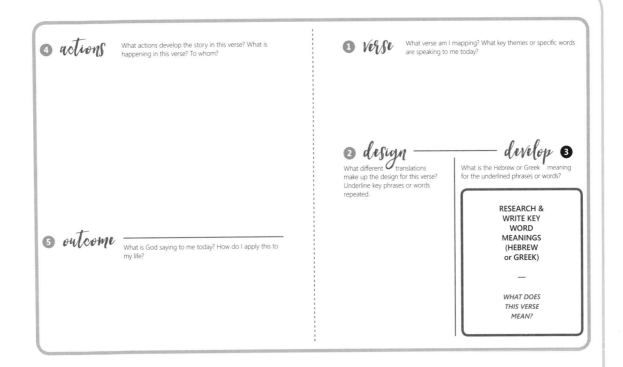

④ *actions* What actions develop the story in this verse? What is happening in this verse? To whom?

① *verse* What verse am I mapping? What key themes or specific words are speaking to me today?

② *design* ——————— *develop* ③

What different translations make up the design for this verse? Underline key phrases or words repeated.

What is the Hebrew or Greek meaning for the underlined phrases or words?

RESEARCH & WRITE KEY WORD MEANINGS (HEBREW or GREEK)

—

WHAT DOES THIS VERSE MEAN?

⑤ *outcome* —————— What is God saying to me today? How do I apply this to my life?

③ *develop*

Develop why and how the verse, key word(s), or idea is important through Hebrew (Old Testament) or Greek (New Testament) word research, definitions, and comparisons. Dig deeper. Use a concordance and online word search databases. Look up the meanings of your key words or phrases and write them down.

Note word choice, part(s) of speech, and find some seriously cool context around your verse.

If a word is used across all translations, find out why. If the verse moves from past tense (something that's already happened) to present tense (something that's ongoing), find out why. If a Greek word was used in one translation and not another . . . find out why.

● **Old Testament verses**—research the Hebrew.

> **Example:** S. 6213. *asah* (aw-saw) a primitive root; to do or make, in the broadest sense and widest application (as follows):—accomplish, advance, appoint

● **New Testament verses**—research the Greek.

> **Example:** S. 4100. *pisteuó* (pist-yoo'-o) from 4102; to have faith (in, upon, or with respect to, a person or thing), i.e. credit; by implication, to entrust (especially one's spiritual well-being to Christ):—believe(-r), commit (to trust), put in trust with

> Note: S. is an abbreviation for *The NIV Exhaustive Concordance.*

Study Prompt:

> Look at the verse in context. Think like a storyteller—how would you explain what's happening in your verse? Find the five senses in the story—sight, smell, sound, taste, and touch—as if you stepped into the characters' shoes. Look at what occurred before and after your verse. What's happening that caused the action in your verse?

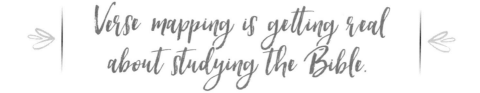

Verse mapping is getting real about studying the Bible.

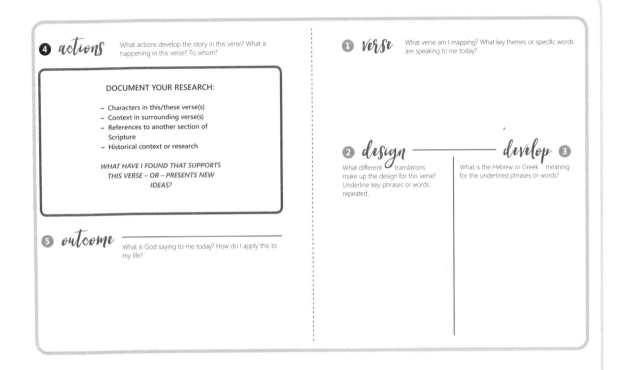

④ actions — What actions develop the story in this verse? What is happening in this verse? To whom?

DOCUMENT YOUR RESEARCH:

– Characters in this/these verse(s)
– Context in surrounding verse(s)
– References to another section of Scripture
– Historical context or research

WHAT HAVE I FOUND THAT SUPPORTS THIS VERSE – OR – PRESENTS NEW IDEAS?

① verse — What verse am I mapping? What key themes or specific words are speaking to me today?

② design ——— develop ③

What different translations make up the design for this verse? Underline key phrases or words repeated.

What is the Hebrew or Greek meaning for the underlined phrases or words?

⑤ outcome — What is God saying to me today? How do I apply this to my life?

④ actions

Actions record:

- What's happening in the verse

- Who the characters are in what you're reading

- How their story relates to other stories/verses/persons in other areas of Scripture

- What are the topics, themes, dates of significant events, and/or theological elements of the verse(s) you're researching

Anything is fair game here, as long as you can back it up with Scripture. Look back a few chapters or verses and read what precedes your verse(s). Identify who, what, where, when. Research the context and customs of what life would have been like for the characters in your verse(s). Look up maps. Open history books. Read about what happened, why it happened, and how it is relevant to your life today.

This is where you'll find how the story connects to *your* story with God. Research it and write it down.

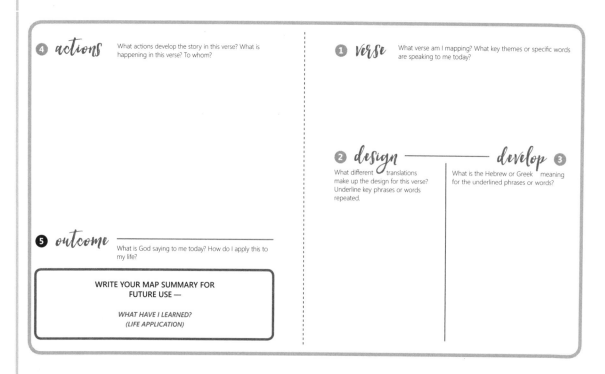

⑤ *outcome*

The *outcome* is a quick-hit summary of what you've learned. One or two sentences should do it. Summarize, jot it down, and come back later to find where the Holy Spirit has confirmed His promises to you. This is your claim on this verse, at this time of your life. The *outcome* should reflect whatever truth has been revealed in your map.

Study Prompt:

As you continue verse mapping, you'll find this is the section that you refer back to most often. Summarize what you've learned—how would you take this truth and apply it in your home, office, school, church, or community? Make it short and powerful.

SPECIAL NOTE

Don't be afraid to start small.

If your first maps are one or two pages with lots of white space, that's okay. Other maps (depending on what you need to hear from God that day) could turn into four pages of study that digs deep into your heart.

Look up a word here. Choose a verse there. Just do it honestly, and the Holy Spirit will grow your passion around His Word. You don't have to have it all figured out with the first or even the twentieth map. You just have to come hungry to the table every day. God will handle the preparation for the feast ahead of time.

I also thought it would be a good idea to share a special map with you—the first one I ever completed when I began verse mapping. To give you a jump-start for your own mapping journey, you'll find an example of a completed map on the following two-page spread for (Acts 2:1-4). Remember that while your map may turn out a little different than mine, this is an example of how the steps help you dig deeper into God's Word and record your progress in the pages of this journal.

So, now it's your turn! Want to give it a try? Join the *community* of other Jesus-chasing mappers out there. Be sure to use the hashtag #VerseMapClub to connect and share your verse-map experience on social media. I'll be adding more posts soon, and you can bet I'll want to see how it's going for you. Connect with me on social media—I'm heart-happy to take this journey with you!

Kristy

4 *actions* — *What if we were never meant to walk our faith journey alone?*

Holy Spirit's ACTIONS to establish the church—

- *Violent wind FILLED the upper room* **(Acts 2:2)**

- *Disciples were FILLED with the Holy Spirit* **(Acts 2:3–4)**

- *Holy Spirit FILLED the COMMUNITY—and each believer—to individual completion* **(Acts 2:4)**

Resulting actions—

- *"every nation" of those gathered hear the rush of WIND* **(Acts 2:5)**

- *Crowds are "utterly amazed" to hear disciples speaking foreign TONGUES* **(Acts 2:7)**

- *Peter stands up to explain what is happening—some 3,000 people come to believe in Christ that day* **(Acts 2:40–41)**

5 *outcome*

Acts is a portrait of COMMUNITY among believers + UNITY with the Holy Spirit. We have the same access to the Holy Spirit that the disciples did; and the same empowering actions for the church to grow.

① *verse* — **ACTS 2:1–4 (NIV)**

When the day of Pentecost came, they were all together in one place. Suddenly a sound like the <u>blowing of a violent wind</u> came from heaven and filled the whole house where they were sitting. They saw what seemed to be <u>tongues of fire</u> that separated and came to rest on each of them. All of them were filled with the Holy Spirit and began to speak in other tongues as the Spirit enabled them.

② *design* —————————— *develop* ③

- **NKJV:** *"And suddenly there came a sound from heaven, as of a <u>rushing mighty wind</u> . . . Then there appeared to them <u>divided tongues, as of fire</u> . . ."*

- **WIND**—*pnoé (S. 4157):*

  "wind"—but wind that comes as a BREATH; a respiration breeze, with gale-force strength

- **FILLED**—*pléroó (S. 4137):*

  "to fill or amply supply; to complete, or fill to individual capacity"

- **FIRE**—*pýr (S. 4442):*

  "fire; a spark or flame." Used figuratively: "God's Spirit—a holy fire, light or lightning, or an eternal flame"

- **TONGUES**—*glóssa (S. 1100):*

  "speech or language"

4 *actions*

What actions develop the story in this verse? What is happening in this verse? To whom?

5 *outcome*

What is God saying to me today? How do I apply this to my life?

1 *verse*   What verse am I mapping? What key themes or specific words are speaking to me today?

2 *design* ——————— *develop* **3**

What different translations make up the design for this verse? Underline key phrases or words repeated.

What is the Hebrew or Greek meaning for the underlined phrases or words?

4 *actions*   What actions develop the story in this verse? What is happening in this verse? To whom?

5 *outcome*

What is God saying to me today? How do I apply this to my life?

1 *verse* What verse am I mapping? What key themes or specific words are speaking to me today?

2 *design* ——————— *develop* **3**

What different translations make up the design for this verse? Underline key phrases or words repeated.

What is the Hebrew or Greek meaning for the underlined phrases or words?

4 *actions*

What actions develop the story in this verse? What is happening in this verse? To whom?

5 *outcome*

What is God saying to me today? How do I apply this to my life?

1 *verse*   What verse am I mapping? What key themes or specific words are speaking to me today?

2 *design* ——————— *develop* **3**

What different ⌢ translations make up the design for this verse? Underline key phrases or words repeated.

What is the Hebrew or Greek ⌢ meaning for the underlined phrases or words?

4  What actions develop the story in this verse? What is happening in this verse? To whom?

5 *outcome* ────────────────

What is God saying to me today? How do I apply this to my life?

1 *verse* What verse am I mapping? What key themes or specific words are speaking to me today?

2 *design* ——————————— *develop* **3**

What different translations make up the design for this verse? Underline key phrases or words repeated.

What is the Hebrew or Greek meaning for the underlined phrases or words?

4 *actions*   What actions develop the story in this verse? What is happening in this verse? To whom?

5 *outcome*

What is God saying to me today? How do I apply this to my life?

1 *verse*

What verse am I mapping? What key themes or specific words are speaking to me today?

2 *design* ——————— *develop* **3**

What different translations make up the design for this verse? Underline key phrases or words repeated.

What is the Hebrew or Greek meaning for the underlined phrases or words?

4 *actions*   What actions develop the story in this verse? What is happening in this verse? To whom?

5 *outcome*

What is God saying to me today? How do I apply this to my life?

1 *verse*   What verse am I mapping? What key themes or specific words are speaking to me today?

2 *design* ———————— *develop* **3**

What different translations make up the design for this verse? Underline key phrases or words repeated.

What is the Hebrew or Greek meaning for the underlined phrases or words?

4 *actions*

What actions develop the story in this verse? What is happening in this verse? To whom?

5 *outcome*

What is God saying to me today? How do I apply this to my life?

1 *verse* What verse am I mapping? What key themes or specific words are speaking to me today?

2 *design* ——————— *develop* **3**

What different translations make up the design for this verse? Underline key phrases or words repeated.

What is the Hebrew or Greek meaning for the underlined phrases or words?

4  What actions develop the story in this verse? What is happening in this verse? To whom?

5 *outcome* ─────────────────

What is God saying to me today? How do I apply this to my life?

1 *verse*   What verse am I mapping? What key themes or specific words are speaking to me today?

2 *design* ———————————— *develop* **3**

What different translations make up the design for this verse? Underline key phrases or words repeated.

What is the Hebrew or Greek meaning for the underlined phrases or words?

4 *actions*

What actions develop the story in this verse? What is happening in this verse? To whom?

5 *outcome*

What is God saying to me today? How do I apply this to my life?

1 *verse*   What verse am I mapping? What key themes or specific words are speaking to me today?

2 *design* ——————— *develop* **3**

What different translations make up the design for this verse? Underline key phrases or words repeated.

What is the Hebrew or Greek meaning for the underlined phrases or words?

4 *actions*

What actions develop the story in this verse? What is happening in this verse? To whom?

5 *outcome*

What is God saying to me today? How do I apply this to my life?

1 *verse*   What verse am I mapping? What key themes or specific words are speaking to me today?

2 *design* —————————— *develop* **3**

What different translations make up the design for this verse? Underline key phrases or words repeated.

What is the Hebrew or Greek meaning for the underlined phrases or words?

4 *actions*   What actions develop the story in this verse? What is happening in this verse? To whom?

5 *outcome* _____

What is God saying to me today? How do I apply this to my life?

1 *verse* What verse am I mapping? What key themes or specific words are speaking to me today?

2 *design* ——————— *develop* **3**

What different translations make up the design for this verse? Underline key phrases or words repeated.

What is the Hebrew or Greek meaning for the underlined phrases or words?

4 *actions*

What actions develop the story in this verse? What is happening in this verse? To whom?

5 *outcome*

What is God saying to me today? How do I apply this to my life?

1 *verse* What verse am I mapping? What key themes or specific words are speaking to me today?

2 *design* ———————————— *develop* **3**

What different translations make up the design for this verse? Underline key phrases or words repeated.

What is the Hebrew or Greek meaning for the underlined phrases or words?

4 *actions*   What actions develop the story in this verse? What is
happening in this verse? To whom?

5 *outcome*

What is God saying to me today? How do I apply this to
my life?

1 *verse*   What verse am I mapping? What key themes or specific words are speaking to me today?

2 *design* —————————— *develop* **3**

What different translations make up the design for this verse? Underline key phrases or words repeated.

What is the Hebrew or Greek meaning for the underlined phrases or words?

4 *actions*

What actions develop the story in this verse? What is happening in this verse? To whom?

5 *outcome*

What is God saying to me today? How do I apply this to my life?

1 *verse*

What verse am I mapping? What key themes or specific words are speaking to me today?

2 *design* ———————— *develop* **3**

What different translations make up the design for this verse? Underline key phrases or words repeated.

What is the Hebrew or Greek meaning for the underlined phrases or words?

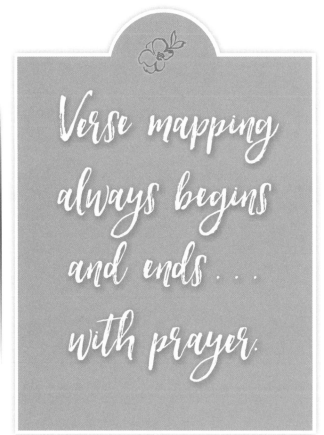

Verse mapping always begins and ends . . . with prayer.

What would it look like if we really needed the Word of God in a way that isn't a chore but a gift with every new day, and were willing to sacrifice to do what it says?

4
What actions develop the story in this verse? What is happening in this verse? To whom?

5 *outcome*
What is God saying to me today? How do I apply this to my life?

1 *verse*

What verse am I mapping? What key themes or specific words are speaking to me today?

2 *design* —————————————— *develop* **3**

What different translations make up the design for this verse? Underline key phrases or words repeated.

What is the Hebrew or Greek meaning for the underlined phrases or words?

4    What actions develop the story in this verse? What is happening in this verse? To whom?

5 *outcome* ——————————————————

What is God saying to me today? How do I apply this to my life?

1 *verse* — What verse am I mapping? What key themes or specific words are speaking to me today?

2 *design* ———————— *develop* **3**

What different translations make up the design for this verse? Underline key phrases or words repeated.

What is the Hebrew or Greek meaning for the underlined phrases or words?

4 *actions*
What actions develop the story in this verse? What is happening in this verse? To whom?

5 *outcome*
What is God saying to me today? How do I apply this to my life?

1 *verse* What verse am I mapping? What key themes or specific words are speaking to me today?

2 *design* ———————— *develop* **3**

What different translations make up the design for this verse? Underline key phrases or words repeated.

What is the Hebrew or Greek meaning for the underlined phrases or words?

4 *actions*

What actions develop the story in this verse? What is happening in this verse? To whom?

5 *outcome*

What is God saying to me today? How do I apply this to my life?

1 *verse*   What verse am I mapping? What key themes or specific words are speaking to me today?

2 *design* ——————————— *develop* **3**

What different translations make up the design for this verse? Underline key phrases or words repeated.

What is the Hebrew or Greek meaning for the underlined phrases or words?

4 *actions*   What actions develop the story in this verse? What is
happening in this verse? To whom?

5 *outcome* _____

What is God saying to me today? How do I apply this to
my life?

1 *verse*   What verse am I mapping? What key themes or specific words are speaking to me today?

2 *design* ———————————— *develop* **3**

What different translations make up the design for this verse? Underline key phrases or words repeated.

What is the Hebrew or Greek meaning for the underlined phrases or words?

4 *actions*

What actions develop the story in this verse? What is happening in this verse? To whom?

5 *outcome*

What is God saying to me today? How do I apply this to my life?

1 *verse*   What verse am I mapping? What key themes or specific words are speaking to me today?

2 *design* ———————————— *develop* **3**

What different translations make up the design for this verse? Underline key phrases or words repeated.

What is the Hebrew or Greek meaning for the underlined phrases or words?

4 *actions*

What actions develop the story in this verse? What is happening in this verse? To whom?

5 *outcome*

What is God saying to me today? How do I apply this to my life?

1 *verse*   What verse am I mapping? What key themes or specific words are speaking to me today?

2 *design* ——————— *develop* **3**

What different translations make up the design for this verse? Underline key phrases or words repeated.

What is the Hebrew or Greek meaning for the underlined phrases or words?

4 *actions*

What actions develop the story in this verse? What is happening in this verse? To whom?

5 *outcome*

_____

What is God saying to me today? How do I apply this to my life?

1 *verse*
What verse am I mapping? What key themes or specific words are speaking to me today?

2 *design* ——————— *develop* **3**

What different translations make up the design for this verse? Underline key phrases or words repeated.

What is the Hebrew or Greek meaning for the underlined phrases or words?

4 *actions*

What actions develop the story in this verse? What is happening in this verse? To whom?

5 *outcome*

What is God saying to me today? How do I apply this to my life?

1 *verse* What verse am I mapping? What key themes or specific words are speaking to me today?

2 *design* —————————————— *develop* **3**

What different translations make up the design for this verse? Underline key phrases or words repeated.

What is the Hebrew or Greek meaning for the underlined phrases or words?

4  What actions develop the story in this verse? What is happening in this verse? To whom?

5 *outcome* ───────────────

What is God saying to me today? How do I apply this to my life?

1 *verse*

What verse am I mapping? What key themes or specific words are speaking to me today?

2 *design* ———————— *develop* **3**

What different translations make up the design for this verse? Underline key phrases or words repeated.

What is the Hebrew or Greek meaning for the underlined phrases or words?

4 *actions*

What actions develop the story in this verse? What is happening in this verse? To whom?

5 *outcome*

What is God saying to me today? How do I apply this to my life?

1 *verse*   What verse am I mapping? What key themes or specific words are speaking to me today?

2 *design* ———————————— *develop* **3**

What different translations make up the design for this verse? Underline key phrases or words repeated.

What is the Hebrew or Greek meaning for the underlined phrases or words?

4 *actions*

What actions develop the story in this verse? What is happening in this verse? To whom?

5 *outcome*

What is God saying to me today? How do I apply this to my life?

1 *verse*   What verse am I mapping? What key themes or specific words are speaking to me today?

2 *design* —————————— *develop* **3**

What different translations make up the design for this verse? Underline key phrases or words repeated.

What is the Hebrew or Greek meaning for the underlined phrases or words?

4 *actions*

What actions develop the story in this verse? What is happening in this verse? To whom?

5 *outcome*

What is God saying to me today? How do I apply this to my life?

1 *verse* What verse am I mapping? What key themes or specific words are speaking to me today?

2 *design* —————————————— *develop* **3**

What different translations make up the design for this verse? Underline key phrases or words repeated.

What is the Hebrew or Greek meaning for the underlined phrases or words?

4 *actions*   What actions develop the story in this verse? What is happening in this verse? To whom?

5 *outcome*

What is God saying to me today? How do I apply this to my life?

1 *verse* What verse am I mapping? What key themes or specific words are speaking to me today?

2 *design* ———————— *develop* **3**

What different translations make up the design for this verse? Underline key phrases or words repeated.

What is the Hebrew or Greek meaning for the underlined phrases or words?

My failure in one area brought us to God's absolute majesty in another.

Time spent verse mapping will draw us closer to Him in every season of our faith-walk.

4 *actions*

What actions develop the story in this verse? What is happening in this verse? To whom?

5 *outcome*

What is God saying to me today? How do I apply this to my life?

1 *verse* What verse am I mapping? What key themes or specific words are speaking to me today?

2 *design* —————————————— *develop* **3**

What different translations make up the design for this verse? Underline key phrases or words repeated.

What is the Hebrew or Greek meaning for the underlined phrases or words?

4 *actions*   What actions develop the story in this verse? What is
happening in this verse? To whom?

5 *outcome*
What is God saying to me today? How do I apply this to
my life?

1 *verse* What verse am I mapping? What key themes or specific words are speaking to me today?

2 *design* ——————————— *develop* **3**

What different translations make up the design for this verse? Underline key phrases or words repeated.

What is the Hebrew or Greek meaning for the underlined phrases or words?

4
What actions develop the story in this verse? What is happening in this verse? To whom?

5 *outcome* _____
What is God saying to me today? How do I apply this to my life?

1 *verse*   What verse am I mapping? What key themes or specific words are speaking to me today?

2 *design* ———————————— *develop* **3**

What different translations make up the design for this verse? Underline key phrases or words repeated.

What is the Hebrew or Greek meaning for the underlined phrases or words?

4 *actions*   What actions develop the story in this verse? What is happening in this verse? To whom?

5 *outcome*

What is God saying to me today? How do I apply this to my life?

1 *verse* What verse am I mapping? What key themes or specific words are speaking to me today?

2 *design* ———————————— *develop* **3**

What different translations make up the design for this verse? Underline key phrases or words repeated.

What is the Hebrew or Greek meaning for the underlined phrases or words?

4 *actions*   What actions develop the story in this verse? What is happening in this verse? To whom?

5 *outcome* ─────────────────────

What is God saying to me today? How do I apply this to my life?

1 *verse*

What verse am I mapping? What key themes or specific words are speaking to me today?

2 *design* ——————— *develop* **3**

What different translations make up the design for this verse? Underline key phrases or words repeated.

What is the Hebrew or Greek meaning for the underlined phrases or words?

4 *actions*

What actions develop the story in this verse? What is happening in this verse? To whom?

5 *outcome*

What is God saying to me today? How do I apply this to my life?

1 *verse*

What verse am I mapping? What key themes or specific words are speaking to me today?

2 *design* —————————— *develop* **3**

What different translations make up the design for this verse? Underline key phrases or words repeated.

What is the Hebrew or Greek meaning for the underlined phrases or words?

4 *actions*   What actions develop the story in this verse? What is happening in this verse? To whom?

5 *outcome* _____

What is God saying to me today? How do I apply this to my life?

1 *verse* What verse am I mapping? What key themes or specific words are speaking to me today?

2 *design* ——————————————— *develop* **3**

What different translations make up the design for this verse? Underline key phrases or words repeated.

What is the Hebrew or Greek meaning for the underlined phrases or words?

4  What actions develop the story in this verse? What is happening in this verse? To whom?

5 *outcome*

What is God saying to me today? How do I apply this to my life?

1 *verse* What verse am I mapping? What key themes or specific words are speaking to me today?

2 *design* ——————— *develop* **3**

What different translations make up the design for this verse? Underline key phrases or words repeated.

What is the Hebrew or Greek meaning for the underlined phrases or words?

4 *actions*

What actions develop the story in this verse? What is happening in this verse? To whom?

5 *outcome*

What is God saying to me today? How do I apply this to my life?

1 *verse*   What verse am I mapping? What key themes or specific words are speaking to me today?

2 *design* ——————— *develop* **3**

What different translations make up the design for this verse? Underline key phrases or words repeated.

What is the Hebrew or Greek meaning for the underlined phrases or words?

4

What actions develop the story in this verse? What is happening in this verse? To whom?

5 *outcome*

What is God saying to me today? How do I apply this to my life?

1 *verse*   What verse am I mapping? What key themes or specific words are speaking to me today?

2 *design* ———————— *develop* **3**

What different translations make up the design for this verse? Underline key phrases or words repeated.

What is the Hebrew or Greek meaning for the underlined phrases or words?

4 *actions*   What actions develop the story in this verse? What is
happening in this verse? To whom?

5 *outcome* _____

What is God saying to me today? How do I apply this to
my life?

1 *verse*   What verse am I mapping? What key themes or specific words are speaking to me today?

2 *design* ——————————— *develop* **3**

What different translations make up the design for this verse? Underline key phrases or words repeated.

What is the Hebrew or Greek meaning for the underlined phrases or words?

4 *actions*   What actions develop the story in this verse? What is happening in this verse? To whom?

5 *outcome*

What is God saying to me today? How do I apply this to my life?

1 *verse*   What verse am I mapping? What key themes or specific words
are speaking to me today?

2 *design* ———————— *develop* **3**

What different ⌒ translations
make up the design for this verse?
Underline key phrases or words
repeated.

What is the Hebrew or Greek   meaning
for the underlined phrases or words?

4 *actions*   What actions develop the story in this verse? What is
happening in this verse? To whom?

5 *outcome*
What is God saying to me today? How do I apply this to
my life?

1 *verse* What verse am I mapping? What key themes or specific words are speaking to me today?

2 *design* ——————— *develop* **3**

What different translations make up the design for this verse? Underline key phrases or words repeated.

What is the Hebrew or Greek meaning for the underlined phrases or words?

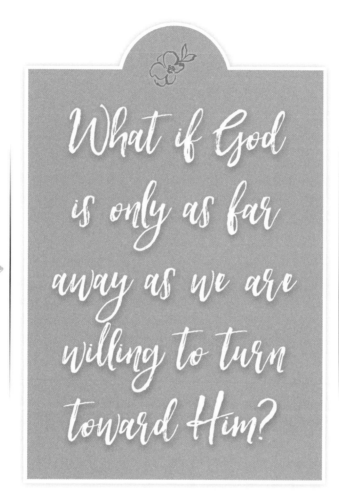

What if God is only as far away as we are willing to turn toward Him?

Verse mapping reveals our personal story roads with the Holy Spirit, just as it reveals deep truths in Scripture.

4 *actions*

What actions develop the story in this verse? What is happening in this verse? To whom?

5 *outcome*

What is God saying to me today? How do I apply this to my life?

1 *verse*   What verse am I mapping? What key themes or specific words are speaking to me today?

2 *design* ———————————— *develop* **3**

What different translations make up the design for this verse? Underline key phrases or words repeated.

What is the Hebrew or Greek meaning for the underlined phrases or words?

4 *actions*   What actions develop the story in this verse? What is happening in this verse? To whom?

5 *outcome* _____

What is God saying to me today? How do I apply this to my life?

1 *verse* What verse am I mapping? What key themes or specific words are speaking to me today?

2 *design* ———————— *develop* **3**

What different translations make up the design for this verse? Underline key phrases or words repeated.

What is the Hebrew or Greek meaning for the underlined phrases or words?

4  What actions develop the story in this verse? What is happening in this verse? To whom?

5 *outcome* _____

What is God saying to me today? How do I apply this to my life?

1 *verse* What verse am I mapping? What key themes or specific words are speaking to me today?

2 *design* —————————— *develop* **3**

What different translations make up the design for this verse? Underline key phrases or words repeated.

What is the Hebrew or Greek meaning for the underlined phrases or words?

4 *actions*   What actions develop the story in this verse? What is happening in this verse? To whom?

5 *outcome*

What is God saying to me today? How do I apply this to my life?

1 *verse* What verse am I mapping? What key themes or specific words are speaking to me today?

2 *design* ——————— *develop* **3**

What different translations make up the design for this verse? Underline key phrases or words repeated.

What is the Hebrew or Greek meaning for the underlined phrases or words?

4  What actions develop the story in this verse? What is happening in this verse? To whom?

5 *outcome* _____

What is God saying to me today? How do I apply this to my life?

1 *verse*   What verse am I mapping? What key themes or specific words are speaking to me today?

2 *design* ———————— *develop* **3**

What different translations make up the design for this verse? Underline key phrases or words repeated.

What is the Hebrew or Greek meaning for the underlined phrases or words?

4 *actions*

What actions develop the story in this verse? What is
happening in this verse? To whom?

5 *outcome*

What is God saying to me today? How do I apply this to
my life?

1 *verse* What verse am I mapping? What key themes or specific words are speaking to me today?

2 *design* ———————— *develop* **3**

What different translations make up the design for this verse? Underline key phrases or words repeated.

What is the Hebrew or Greek meaning for the underlined phrases or words?

4  What actions develop the story in this verse? What is happening in this verse? To whom?

5 *outcome* _____

What is God saying to me today? How do I apply this to my life?

1 *verse*   What verse am I mapping? What key themes or specific words are speaking to me today?

2 *design* ——————— *develop* **3**

What different translations make up the design for this verse? Underline key phrases or words repeated.

What is the Hebrew or Greek meaning for the underlined phrases or words?

4 *actions*   What actions develop the story in this verse? What is happening in this verse? To whom?

5 *outcome* _____

What is God saying to me today? How do I apply this to my life?

1 *verse* What verse am I mapping? What key themes or specific words are speaking to me today?

2 *design* —————————— *develop* **3**

What different translations make up the design for this verse? Underline key phrases or words repeated.

What is the Hebrew or Greek meaning for the underlined phrases or words?

4  What actions develop the story in this verse? What is happening in this verse? To whom?

5 *outcome*

What is God saying to me today? How do I apply this to my life?

1 *verse* What verse am I mapping? What key themes or specific words are speaking to me today?

2 *design* ——————— *develop* **3**

What different translations make up the design for this verse? Underline key phrases or words repeated.

What is the Hebrew or Greek meaning for the underlined phrases or words?

4 *actions*   What actions develop the story in this verse? What is happening in this verse? To whom?

5 *outcome*

What is God saying to me today? How do I apply this to my life?

1 *verse* What verse am I mapping? What key themes or specific words are speaking to me today?

2 *design* ——————— *develop* **3**

What different translations make up the design for this verse? Underline key phrases or words repeated.

What is the Hebrew or Greek meaning for the underlined phrases or words?

4  What actions develop the story in this verse? What is happening in this verse? To whom?

5 *outcome* ——————————————
What is God saying to me today? How do I apply this to my life?

1 *verse*   What verse am I mapping? What key themes or specific words are speaking to me today?

2 *design* —————————————— *develop* **3**

What different translations make up the design for this verse? Underline key phrases or words repeated.

What is the Hebrew or Greek meaning for the underlined phrases or words?

4

What actions develop the story in this verse? What is happening in this verse? To whom?

5 *outcome*

What is God saying to me today? How do I apply this to my life?

1 *verse* What verse am I mapping? What key themes or specific words are speaking to me today?

2 *design* ——————— *develop* **3**

What different translations make up the design for this verse? Underline key phrases or words repeated.

What is the Hebrew or Greek meaning for the underlined phrases or words?

4 *actions*

What actions develop the story in this verse? What is happening in this verse? To whom?

5 *outcome*

What is God saying to me today? How do I apply this to my life?

1 *verse*   What verse am I mapping? What key themes or specific words are speaking to me today?

2 *design* ——————————— *develop* **3**

What different translations make up the design for this verse? Underline key phrases or words repeated.

What is the Hebrew or Greek meaning for the underlined phrases or words?

VERSE MAPPING STUDY PLANS

In our Verse Mapping Bible studies (such as: Verse Mapping Luke and Verse Mapping Acts), you'll find mapping journeys through a specific book of the Bible to gather and study along with a small group, or to learn during your own self-study time. But what about the seasons in our journey with God where a more thematic approach might be what we're looking for?

We've given you examples of thematic studies below—Faith, Parables, or Healing topics recorded in the Gospel of Luke and Miracles, Prayer, or Ministry topics recorded in the book of Acts. Depending upon where your heart is and where the Holy Spirit leads you, you might want to study themes in the Bible that cross over multiple books. Maybe you'd like to research the miracles of Jesus recorded in the Gospels. Map the promises of God found in the Psalms. To explore relationships, dig deep into topics like forgiveness, reconciliation, or grace, and map the verses you find. Or study themes around specific times of the calendar year—the coming of Christ during the Advent season or the Passover around Easter.

Whatever maps you choose to record in this journal, remember that the journey doesn't end with one page. Your mapping journey through the Bible continues from book to book, theme to theme. . . and year over year, each time you gather with God.

on FAITH:

- Luke 5:12–14
- Luke 5:17–26
- Luke 5:27–28
- Luke 7:36–39
- Luke 9:18–20
- Luke 18:35–43

on PARABLES:

- Luke 8:4–8
- Luke 8:16
- Luke 10:25–37
- Luke 13:18–19
- Luke 15:1–7
- Luke 15:11–31

on HEALING:

- Luke 4:31–37
- Luke 5:12–16
- Luke 5:40–41
- Luke 8:46–48
- Luke 13:10–17
- Luke 18:35–43

VERSE MAPPING STUDY PLANS

Ready to feast again? Bring your verse mapping journal and gather with God in a new mapping journey! Feasting on the Abundance study plans for the book of Acts are here:

on MIRACLES:

- Acts 2:1–4
- Acts 5:19–20
- Acts 9:36–42
- Acts 12:7
- Acts 16:17–19
- Acts 20:9–12

on PRAYER:

- Acts 1:13–14
- Acts 8:15–16
- Acts 10:2–6
- Acts 11:5–9
- Acts 14:22–23
- Acts 22:17–21

on MINISTRY:

- Acts 4:29
- Acts 6:3–4
- Acts 13:2–3
- Acts 16:6–10
- Acts 23:11
- Acts 27:13–26

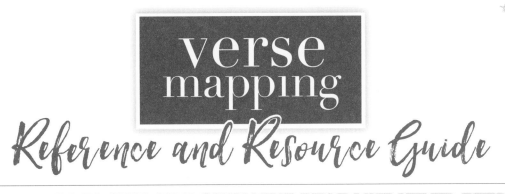

verse mapping
Reference and Resource Guide

RESOURCES TO HELP YOU STUDY THE BIBLE LIKE NEVER BEFORE

BOOKS

- *The NKJV Study Bible, 2nd Edition* (Thomas Nelson), by Earl D. Radmacher (editor), Ronald B. Allen (editor), H. Wayne House (editor)

- *NIV Chronological Study Bible* (Thomas Nelson)

- *NIV Biblical Theology Study Bible* (Zondervan), D. A. Carson (general editor)

- *The NIV Exhaustive Bible Concordance, Third Edition: A Better Strong's Bible Concordance* (Zondervan), by John R. Kohlenberger III

- *Mounce's Complete Expository Dictionary of Old and New Testament Words* (Zondervan), by William D. Mounce (general editor)

- Concordance, if other biblical translations are preferred (NASB, KJV, MSG, etc.)

- Other Bible studies—these books/study guides that are gathering dust on the shelves could be a gold mine of information when researching. Get them out and use them!

WEBSITES

- BibleGateway.com—free biblical translations, Hebrew/Greek lexicon, commentaries, concordance(s), biblical dictionaries

- BibleHub.com—great word search site, Hebrew/Greek lexicon

- Logos.com—free and paid in-depth biblical resource site

- YouTube.com—videos of sites/locations being researched

*ALWAYS utilize references/websites that come from reputable sources (i.e., NOT an online crowd-sourcing encyclopedia). It is okay to use whatever websites pop up in a Google search—as long as they contain evidence you can confirm. Approved websites could be, for example: university/seminary websites, or sites that contain articles from recognized research/news sources (History.com, Smithsonian, National Geographic, museums or historical institutions, etc.).

HISTORY BOOKS AND MAPS

Your local library can be an invaluable resource for:

- Greco-Roman art, archaeology, and history books

- Maps and in-depth historical context on life and culture in a first-century Roman world

- Anything that includes timelines, maps, etc. of the ancient world will add to your research

The point of all of this is to **think like a researcher.** *Be curious. Ask questions. Dig for answers. Don't just accept an answer—use it as a springboard to research on your own.*

SMALL GROUP OR CHURCH MEMBERS/LEADERS

- Someone who is seminary trained by education/vocation

- Someone who has walked with Jesus for many years—even in ministry—and may have valuable insight into the topic you're researching

- A member who has studied Hebrew/Greek (wowza, if you do!)—or Jewish culture

- Someone who learned what you're discussing in another Bible study

Bottom line—use the resources/sphere of influence within your reach!
ASK QUESTIONS. Own your faith in Jesus; the learning is up to you. :-)

Community Connections

Need more help? Go to versemapping.com or search the following social media hashtags to find other mappers who've shared their mapping journeys online. You'll find support and collaboration in a space that's always available.

#VerseMapping

#VerseMapclub

#GoandMakeChallenge (community maps from *Luke: Gathering the Goodness of God's Word*)

#FeastandFullChallenge (community maps from *Acts: Feasting on the Abundance of God's Word*)

⇒ Acknowledgments ⇐

When I picture a feast table—a rugged, backyard dream that became this verse mapping journey—I see rows of chairs that are no longer empty. I see place-settings that are filled, smiles that are warm, and a celebration dinner that couldn't have been if not for those gathered around this project.

For the friends who believed in this journey enough to invite us into it: John Raymond, Rachelle Gardner, Daisy Hutton . . .

For the friends and mentors who helped set the stage and lay the table: Katherine and Sarah, Beth, Jeane, Colleen, Bex, Allen, Sharon, Maggie, Eileen, Marlene, Kerry, Joyce, Kelli, Gary and Lanette . . .

For the incredible editorial team who saw to every detail of this feast in the Word: Mark Weising, Sara Riemersma, Robin Crosslin, and Greg Clouse . . .

For the beloved who sit closest at the table: Rick and Linda, Jenny, Jeremy, Brady, Carson, and Colt . . .

And for the One who pulls out the chair and waits for us . . .

. . . You showed up. You gave. You stayed and you changed everything about the journey. For that—*and for you*—I am profoundly grateful. I love you.

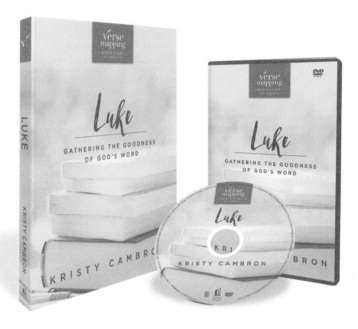